Poetry By
Gregory "Crash" Cooper

Produced by:

FriesenPress

Suite 300 – 852 Fort Street
Victoria, BC, Canada V8W 1H8

www.friesenpress.com

Distributed to the trade by The Ingram Book Company

DEDICATION

I dedicate this book to my Mom who is my advocate
and supporter through good times and difficult times.

FORWARD

Poetry often is a glimpse into a poet's soul, a poet's innermost feelings, values, beliefs and thoughts. Poetry also can be a vehicle for self-examination that allows one to confront individual and societal concerns and worries as well as the everyday dilemmas of life. Poems written by teens can be passages to adulthood and later in life can serve as time machines to the past and glances into the future.

Greg Cooper wrote his poetry as a teenager. His innermost thoughts and reflections are contained in these pages. Greg's poems serve as a testament to his growth and development as a young man and his willingness, courage and perseverance when facing the daily challenges and angst of teenage life. He did so with humility, care and thoughtfulness. No topic was excluded. Read these pages and discover the essence of the person Greg was to become — a caring, reflective adult not afraid to think about and act upon the problems, issues and tests of modern day life. *Bruce Seney, Faculty Advisor, University of British Columbia,* **Greg's teacher at London Junior and Steveston Senior Secondary Schools**

Greg writes of souls in high risk situations, even in the most commonplace settings. Just when you think these poems will leave you in despair, at once you are snatched away and see a glimmer of hope. You see the risk, although terrifying at times, as just ordinary; it is the hope that is singular and everlasting.

Greg places us in physical danger, in mental danger, and in spiritual danger. He writes of innocence, but questions it in order to explore what lies beneath. Throughout, he ultimately remains an optimist despite daring to venture into these dark corners of existence. He paints a world that few would acknowledge: raw, honest, and flawed. He takes us on a shared journey through multiple extremes of human experience; yet, our reflections at the end are satisfying, united, and at peace.
Sandra Birrell, President of The National CCSVI Society (NCS)

INTRODUCTION

I have memories of days gone by
When I was healthy and determined to try
And I'm quite surprised to still be alive.

I miss my life the way it was
I don't remember how it was or when it changed.
And it just occurred to me that I
Have experienced/endured a rather great
Transformation in my life.

Written May 20, 2012

I wrote my poetry as a teenager, years prior to being diagnosed with Multiple Sclerosis (MS) in 1997 and Chronic Cerebrospinal Venous Insufficiency (CCSVI) and a Seizure Disorder, both in 2010. Some of my poems foreshadow the challenges I am confronted with daily.

A portion of the sale of each book will be donated to The National CCSVI Society (NCS). My email address is greg.cooper1971@ yahoo.ca or find me on Facebook: Greg Cooper, Ladner, British Columbia. Love to hear from you.

Greg "Crash" Cooper

SPECIAL THANKS

I am grateful and wish to acknowledge my appreciation for the dedication, contributions, efforts and tenacious assistance of my Aunt Penny Stepler, my Uncle Peter Stoffels and my friend Pat Popek. And most of all I thank my Mom, Bev Bentley, and my Aunt, Peggy Bentley without whom my poetry would never have been published. Their perseverance and encouragement through all aspects of publishing my book was Herculean.

I thank Bruce Seney and Sandra Birrell for their kind Forward.

A special thanks to those who read and graciously commented on my poetry.

To all who will read my poems, "Thanks, Eh!"

ACKNOWLEDGEMENTS

Cover layout by Patrick Popek
of Gonzo Records and Popek Photography

Back cover photo by Shannon Leigh (Blair) Dickinson
of Shannon Leigh Photography.ca

COMMENTS

Greg's language skills were always beyond expectations for his age. He is my nephew born on my 21st Birthday and is an Aquarian. I am so thankful that Greg decided to write his insightful poems putting the feelings and thoughts, roiling through his mind, into words that we can all relate to no matter what our age. Today, Greg spreads his positive outlook with all who he meets leaving everyone with a smile. Sharing his poetry means many more will revisit those times of growing pains and joys. Thank you Greg!
Peggy Bentley

Greg's poetry emanates deep understanding, with insight and knowledge towards the emotional journey we are all on. Greg "freely" shares his emotions with others: his generosity has left many with a smile. I have appreciated Greg's wisdom in my life. I know many will benefit from his poetry.
Julie McAtasney, Friend and Supporter

Every morning I see you, there's a smile on your face.
The invisible between us is a happy space.
I've known you for almost three years.
We've been through laughter, heartache and tears.

You've taught me to sing every song I've heard
And both of us know that "WAH" is the word.
You've taught me patience and how to be strong
With a friend like you, How could I go wrong.

Everything you've given, I gave back to you
You're a gift in my life for all that you do
If there's one thing I know that will never end
Till the end of time you will be my friend.

Honesty and trust is something we've earned
"To just be myself" is from you I have learned
Thank you Greg — you are an amazing man.
Never say I can't cuz I know you can!
Poem from Julie McAtasney to Greg — February 13, 2004

Greg speaks so eloquently of the angst of youth. Those of us who knew Greg at this time......mainly 1986/7, 15 and 16 years old, might be surprised to discover this talent and the abundance with which he expressed it. Some of these writings come to a conclusion and some leave us to ponder our own conclusion. All leave little doubt as to a teenager exploring the world as he sees it and confronting it.................thought provoking work, Greg.
Marilynne Bell

These poems are evidence of Greg's nature which is to look for the beauty and humor in life. His illness has given him daily challenges that all would struggle with. However, within Greg there is always the willingness to find something that is good, beautiful or humorous. He is a survivor and his willingness to see beauty in his life and others is what I admire.
Romayne Gallagher MD, CCFPHead, Divisions of Palliative and Residential Care Department of Family and Community Medicine Providence Health Care Clinical Professor, Division of Palliative Care, UBC

When I knew Greg he was a deep and serious person. His caring and thoughtfulness were ever present. He would leave me notes with poetry that never ceased to amaze me about how he could reveal the depths of his soul with such evocative words. Wishing all the best!
Alexis Hill

Greg has always had a way with words and a knack for illustrative expression through prose; his mastery of linguistic contortions is of magnanimous proportions as he weaves his unique tales of life with wit and humour and raw, yet simple and poignant accuracy. His poetry, for me, is matched by no other I've ever known, or will ever, know.
Shannon Leigh (Blair) Dickinson, RSW BSW BA

I met Greg in 1984. I had just moved to a new city and was entering a new high school in which I knew no one. Greg was one of the first friends I made and we had an instant bond through the love of two things, Led Zeppelin and writing poetry. In those days we had little life experience but when we combined a little marijuana with a back drop of Zeppelin and a pen to paper we often struck allegorical gold. I have Greg to thank for helping me forge my own creativity in those days and I'm glad to know that he has kept up with it.
Farrell McLaughlin

Greg and I became fast friends when we met in our first photography class at London Jr. Secondary. As we conquered the darkroom together, Greg even applied his creative depth to developing techniques we could use to respectfully deal with farts that would happen in the middle of 'process' - what laugh riots we had together! Mr. Lorenz's field trips and yearbook shooting were only a start as the hanging out would continue at Greg's place with the rest of our crew and that great trampoline.

Some ten years after discovering Greg's tragic condition at our high school reunion, I was inspired to play 'Ten Years Gone' by Led Zeppelin. As I dove into this tune, memories of the old days came rushing back for it was Greg who first introduced me to Led Zeppelin in grade 9 - hearing Zep II and Jimmy Page for the first time changed my life - all thanks to Greg.

This emotional event in 2008 spurred me to look up my old chum, and when we met again, I was surprised to learn that at the time Greg was feverishly writing away in the wee hours of

the night, discovering his voice and reflecting everything in his life on paper - I had no clue! It seems this was a most private endeavour. But it thrills me to bits that all these years later, Greg gets to see his poems published in this beautiful book. The spirit of that kid I knew continues to live in Greg's soul today everytime I see him throw his head back in raucous laughter...how not?!
Pat Popek

Greg, I met you back in high school when your fluorescent personality bounded into the Photography classroom with more life than I had ever seen before. I was drawn to you immediately. We spent countless hours pondering life and the meaning of it all while out on "assignment". Being on assignment for us usually meant a stop at Big Scoop for coffee while we procrastinated about our work. Your sensitive and caring personality shows through your poetry and I feel privileged to be one of the first to read your poems before publication. Thank you for sharing a little bit of your "teenaged" self with me....you made me feel young all over again! I love you!
Angela Shoemaker

Ever since first meeting Greg Cooper in Grade 8 (1984), I've found him to be a cheerful, vibrant, creative, and beautiful person. These traits resonate through his poems, and fill me with reminiscent joy every time I read them.
Chris Iversen, B. Ed

I can remember hours of our time being spent on the trampoline in Greg's backyard. Greg would always create games or scenes from his imagination to act out which provided the backdrop to our afternoons. Later, when music replaced the trampoline, I'd watch as Greg would lean back and close his eyes and become 'lost' in what he was listening to. You could almost see him going into his mind. Once the song was over, he'd return, slowly opening his eyes and smiling and you could see he had gone away and had come back refreshed — as though he'd been on a vacation and seen something no one else had.
Dr. Jonathan McVicar, Ph.D. R.Psych

Greg Cooper is my Super Hero. He is an inspiration to all who know him and an amazing Poet! I am so blessed to be able to call him my friend. I admire his courage, strength and talent.
Janice Whiteside, Owner of Peepers Optical Consultant Ltd.

I've had the pleasure of being Greg's trainer for the past ten years. Through the ups and downs, Greg has always loved his exercise. Greg has won the admiration of all those that watch his determination in the gym. And of course he's won the admiration of his trainer over our many years together. To really know and understand Greg is to read through his poetry. He has taken his experiences in life and his interactions with people and created poems with feeling and emotion.
Murray Phillips, aka Murr Man, Personal Trainer

Greg loves poetry and writes many that are very thought provoking. Spending time with Greg is always a unique experience, a cherished little life event that everyone walks away from as a better person. How often can you say that about someone? You are in our hearts every day, Greg.
Fran and Darrel Harder

Don't let Cooper's seemingly simple diction and structure fool you. Beneath these rhymes is a mastery of emotions...emotions we can all relate to in a universal way. As he states so well in the coda to this sensitive work "I am a collector of Emotion". Readers will be glad he has shared his collection with us.
Phil Menger, Library Technician

Greg's poems brought me back to my teens and young adulthood. The raw emotions! Fear, pain, love, loss, yearning. I too remember trying to make sense of life and death and heaven and hell. I love the shades of hippie philosophy intertwined throughout. What strikes me is his poetry isn't all teen angst and despair. It's full of thoughtful insight and LOVE. Thanks for sharing!
Ginger MacQueen

"Gregory Cooper's collection of Poems is Insightful, Diverse and Fascinating, a touching piece of work from a courageous young man."
Gregory Sandford, B.A.

"By itself love is nothing, a heavy blob of empty feeling. Then a person, a single person heaves it up, suddenly overcome by compassion this person spreads it around...." G. Cooper. So grateful for the friend that I've made, my keeper of secrets, and many times the sun behind the dark clouds. Cheers to you, Crash, and all that you have accomplished.... You Rock!!
Safia Hassan

MEDIA

Following is a list of news paper reports, TV appearances and 2 Documentaries Greg has appeared in reflecting his life since 1997.

1998   -   The Nature of Things, Documentary with Dr. David Suzuki

1998   -   BCTV News, August 25

1998   -   CBC French, December 6, at The Compassion Club in Vancouver BC

2000   -   Illegal Compassion, Documentary by Om Shiva Productions, Capilano College

2001   -   VTV Interview, July 4

2001   -   The Province Newspaper, July 5

2001   -   Richmond Review Newspaper, July 8

2002   -   Global TV News, Crimes of Compassion, February 20

2002   -   Richmond Review, September 8

2007   -   "THE UNION: the business behind getting high", Documentary by Adam Scorgie

2010   -   CTV News, September 17

In 1998 Greg participated in an episode of "The Nature of Things" about Medical Marijuana at the Compassion Club in Vancouver BC with Dr. David Suzuki.

"To Greg: Best wishes:
David Suzuki". *March 20, 2012*

Greg, you were amazing, you were Amazing in the film and you sharing your story has moved and opened minds all over the world. Thank you for taking the time to share your story with us, the film wouldn't be the same without you. You're a hero in our minds. *Adam Scorgie: Filmmaker of the award winning Canadian (BC) Documentary, "THE UNION: the business behind getting-high", 2007.*

Hi Greg — My daughter just had me sit down and watch The Union — she's 15- I have MS — she was impressed by how open you were about MS and marijuana — she was born in Red Deer, AB — though we now live in Michigan. Thank you for being a part of the movie and sharing your experiences. Were we ever shocked when I realized I'm FB Friends w/ your mom, Bev, and have prayed for you during your last two hospital stays! Small world eh? Anyhow, was nice to feel like I know a movie star in a round-about way — you have an AMAZING mom — you are an Amazingly strong man. Keep the Faith! Blessings. **Dana Dernberger, regarding THE UNION.**

OTHER PUBLICATIONS

World Poetry Movement - "Stars in Our Hearts"

Greg, you should be genuinely proud of your accomplishment. Of the thousands of poems we read each year, only a fraction can be published. We are pleased that "The First Love Poem" will be featured in this classic publication.

Again, congratulations, Greg. We feel you have a special talent and look forward to the publication of your poem in Stars in Our Hearts.
Suzanne Hilary, Managing Editor, May 2012

CONTENTS

LOVE:

Valentine's Day — February 13, 1986 9

The First Love Poem — February 14, 1986 11

Love — March 1, 1986 12

Lightning Strikes — April 30, 1986 16

My Girlfriend — May 5, 1986 17

The Light — August 6, 1986 23

What Is Love — August 9, 1986 25

OH, What A Sweet Emotion — August 23, 1986 27

Love Progresses — September 8, 1986 28

The Queen of Hearts — October 18, 1986 29

Remember — October 22, 1986 30

Shelter and Misty Tears — November 3, 1986 31

Sky Blue — November 12, 1986 32

Vibrant Violet — December 14, 1986 34

Another Aspect of Love — December 16, 1986 37

Dazzling — December 31, 1986 39

Limping Cutlery — September 21, 1987 46

One Touch — January 23, 1988 56

Can Ya Feel It? — February 12, 1988 87

The Pains of Happiness — August 17, 1988 94

The Sweetness of the Thunder — August 18, 1988 95

The Ultimate Love — October 2, 1988 97

Departure — October 1988 98

Waiting — December 8, 1988 101

I Follow You — January 8, 1989...................103

My Obsession — January 9, 1989 105

Dedicated to Her Song — January 10, 1989 107

Everything To You — January 26, 1989.............110

This Stranger of Mine — March 13, 1989............116

Lavender Eyes — July 12, 1989 118

Love Haunts — October 13, 1989 124

My Angelic Moon — November 14, 1989 127

She Is Beauty In Turmoil — November 16, 1989 129

I Love You — November 22, 1989 130

Sketches — November 22, 1989 131

Blush — December 3, 1989........................134

A Couple of Comparisons — December 30, 1989 ...138

Skylights — December 30, 1989...................140

Romantic Chance — January 1, 1990 144

Train of Romance — January 4, 1990 147

GIVE ME STRENGTH — January 6, 1990............148

To Alexis, I Love You — January 7, 1990 151

ALEXIS — January 10, 1990 153

It's Ironic But It's True — January 12, 1990..........156

APES — January 17, 1990 165

WIND — Sometime in 1990 172

RELIGION:

A Fallen Angel — January 15, 1986..................3

You Spin A Web — February 4, 1986.................4

Hell — April 25, 1986 15

Forever — July 10, 1986 22

The Verdict — Early-mid 1988 .89

EMOTION:

Darkness — February 8, 1986 5

Dazed and Confused — March 4, 1986 13

Boredom — April 7, 1986 14

Paradise — November 19, 1986 33

Trapped — August 23, 1987 43

I Don't Get It — Late 1987 47

I Wonder — October 31, 1987 48

This Is How It Works — November 2, 1987 49

The Expiation of a Timeless Curse — June 9, 1988 . . .88

RAGE — November 25, 1988 99

SMILES — September 1989 120

Under the Sunshine — November 15, 1989 128

There's a Poetic Verse in a Gold Frame —
November 26, 1989 132

A Sigh's Silence — December 25, 1989 137

Cheated and Swayed — December 30, 1989 139

The Cause of the Swoon — January 1, 1990 142

Alexis — January 1, 1990 143

Presumptuous — January 1, 1990 145

No More Does Hope — January 6, 1990 149

If I Had A Gun — January 16, 1990 164

Is Sanctuary Is Freedom — January 18, 1990 166

Be'in Blunt — January 20, 1990 167

I Am A Collector of Emotion — Sometime in 1990 . . . 173

DRINKING AND DRIVING:

A Bad Dream — February 9, 1986 6

DRUGS:

Drugs — February 9, 1986 8

HIGH — January 7, 1990 152

WHAT IS POETRY?:

Poetry Is — January 14, 1986. 1

Poems of Mine — May 16, 1986 18

Just the Ramblings — July 22, 1988 93

TO PONDER:

Questions — December 14, 1986 35

Originality — Sometime in 1987. 50

Rock and Roll — February 7, 1988 67

Country Lights — December 31, 1989 141

The Candle — January 6, 1990 150

DEATH AND LIFE:

Escape — June 8, 1986 19

Gone — June 10, 1986 21

I Am Alive — March 2, 1987 41

Dreams — August 23, 1987. .44

Ohh, Baby It's Dark — September 2, 1987 45

Beyond Reason? — November 19, 1987. 51

Some What Perplexing? — November 19, 1987 52

Autumn — November 19, 1987. 53

Baptism — January 3, 1988 .54

Humanity's Problem — January 10, 1988 55

My Soul — January 24, 1988 57

The Reason to Mingle — February 1, 1988 58

What If? — February 2, 1988. .59

Ones Next Step — February 3, 1988 60

Shake Your Mind — February 3, 1988 61

Push to Prepare — February 3, 1988 62

A Thought — February 4, 1988 63

Hole New Infinity — February 4, 1988 64

The Inter Zone — February 5, 1988 65

AAAAHH — February 7, 1988 69

STOP — February 7, 1988. 80

Peace, Dove and Feather — February 9, 1988 82

Testimony — July 22, 1988. 91

A Dangerous Moment — August 18, 1988 96

In the Back of My Mind — February 5, 1989. 111

Don't Take Me From My Cloud — February 6, 1989. . .112

In My Bubble, Behind My Wall — March 1, 1989. 114

STAGES — March 1, 1989. 115

The Death of a Secret — October 2, 1989 121

Balance — November 12, 1989. 126

People Are Predictable — January 2, 1990 146

LOGIC — January 12, 1990. .154

Honesty — January 12, 1990 155

Obligation — January 12, 1990 159

Truth — January 12, 1990 158

Opportunities — January 12, 1990 161

It's Obvious — January 12, 1990 162

And Now I'm Gone — January 22, 1990 168

A Relationship in a Cold Winter — January 23, 1990 169

Perspective Blinders — February 7, 1990 171

HUMOUR:

Cow Shoe — June 9, 1986 20

Shining — January 11, 1989 .109

CHRISTMAS:

XMAS — December 1988 100

YOUTH:

Oh Painful Youth — December 8, 1988 102

Youth — November 2, 1989 125

To Be Young — January 12, 1990. 160

Experience — January 14, 1990 163

Why — February 2, 1990 170

Greg, in the many years you have lived in my heart and soul I have learned some important life lessons through you my friend. I am now ready and wise enough to understand and appreciate how life works a bit better, and see where you have been coming from all along.....

Life can be great if you remember to live with:

PERSISTENCE: Know what fulfills you and keep working to get "there". Persist and don't give up!

PASSION: To feel deeply and strongly about something/someone is a gift. Live passionately where and when you can!

DREAMS: Because they put a light in your eye and a spring in your step. Dream always!

Congratulations on publishing your book and realizing one of your dreams!

Love and hugs always!

Allie (Johnson) Foster

"Reach high, for stars lie hidden in your soul. Dream deep for every dream precedes the goal." (Vaull Starr)

Poetry Is

Sweet emotions
Hard distortions
Soft commotions
Bitter devotions
And something to detest
And a passion
Poetry is . . .

A Fallen Angel

Lucifer, in all his glory,
A fallen angel with a story.
He will not rest till the world is blind,
And everyone has lost there mind.
Jesus Christ will interfere,
But, Lucifer, won't shed a tear,
For the Prince of Darknes.
has no fear,
In snaching you up from the rear.
He will take you down to his domain,
Where for all eternity you will Remain.

Written By [signature] Jan 15 86

A Fallen Angel

Lucifer, in all his glory,
A fallen angel with a story.
He will not rest till the world is blind,
And everyone has lost their mind.
Jesus Christ will interfere,
But, Lucifer, won't shed a tear,
For the Prince of Darkness has no fear
In snatching you up from the rear.
He will take you down to his domain,
Where for all eternity you will
Remain.

January 15, 1986

You Spin a Web

You spin a web to catch me dead,

Your black and fiery body said,

For you are the one that I most dread.

I see your image in my head,

And remember the scared words you once said.

If they come for me,

I will be free,

And to you I will owe no fee.

February 4, 1986

Darkness

In the darkness of the night,
Walking on the street is a fright,
You hear the song of the night birds in flight,
And wonder who's watching you in this dark night.
As you walk on faster and faster
you dream of any possible disaster.
You do up your coat nice and tight
so the freezing night air doesn't bite.
Then you see home all lit up and bright
And you know that soon you will be alright.

February 8, 1986

A Bad Dream

Cruising down the highway at 190 mph,
At 2:00 in the morning,
Going heaven knows where,
With a full tank of gas.
Lights in the distance, your mind doesn't see
Closer and closer,
You seem to be blind,
Around a corner they're out of sight,
Come around again, they light up the night.
As you go through them your car disappears.
You're floating in darkness,
A buzz in your ears.
Figures of darkness
Figures of light
Dance all around
Then into the night.
Your mind seems at ease
As you float like a breeze.
Then with screaming pain,
You're awake once again.
With blood all around,
You're sprawled on the ground.
With sirens ahead,
You wish you were dead.
You wake up again,
You're in a strange bed.
Your body aches

Your nerves being raked,
It all seems unreal,
You wish you would heal,
Maybe tomorrow, who knows how you'll feel.
You pray to your god with your appeal,
Maybe someday, better you'll feel.
In the meantime,
Stick it out and be tough.
Drinking and Driving
Sometimes is rough.

February 9, 1986

Drugs

Pop a pill,
Won't make you ill.
Shoot the line,
You'll feel fine.
Take a swig,
Or 6 or 7,
Or maybe 8, won't make you late.
Have a toke, don't just smoke,
Just get High
Cause you will fly.
You fly so high you almost die.
Come around again you're in the rain.
So you feel some pain,
But you still do it again.
You go through hell,
Like the ring of a bell,
But you must be cool,
Not just a fool.

February 9, 1986

Valentine's Day

At Valentine's Day
We have so much fun,
Kissing each other,
Like butter to a bun.
We dance all around,
We have so much fun
Sending cards,
With wishes of love,
To our friends who are dear to our hearts,
Eating candies and little heart shaped tarts,
Ignoring our school,
To be like little fools
Our eyes shine like smooth little pools
And we know today will be just fine.

February 13, 1986

The first Love Poem

Love is above all other emotions.
It cannot be made by somebodies potions.
If you'er in love you surly will know,
Just as the wind surly will blow.
Love is not something, you can just throw away
Love is real, just like the day
If your love is true, it will last forever.
Forget this not, forever never.

Written by Greg Cooper

Feb 14 86

The First Love Poem

Love is above all other emotions.
It cannot be made by somebody's potions.
If you're in love you surely will know,
Just as the wind surely will blow.
Love is not something you can just throw away
Love is real just like the day.
If your love is true, it will last forever.
Forget this not, forever never.

February 14, 1986

LOVE

Try to guess: what is this mess?
A bundle of sorrow wrapped up in happiness.
It's as beautiful as freshly fallen snow,
On a crisp winter's day,
But can get as ugly as anyone can say.
A feeling beyond human comprehension,
An emotion above all others.
A feeling that's sad,
A feeling that's mad,
Or at a different time,
A feeling that's glad.
It can be magic,
Or it might be tragic.
It's a feeling that's trouble,
Or one that'll bubble.
No one can say if it will make the day
Or turn it into a great demented mud puddle.

March 1, 1986

Dazed and Confused

Life's a bitch,
And sometimes it really can itch.
One minute life's dandy,
And plenty of love's handy,
Then wake up one morning
And you're in the ditch.
You *Bleepin* burn with desire
To punch someone's nose
And throw them out into the biting cold snow.
You know you're right,
They say you're wrong
It *Bleepin* stings all night long.
Dazed and Confused,
You get verbally abused,
It really does suck
And it lights a very short fuse.
You're set like a bomb,
To go off at anything that's wrong.
Your temper's short,
You never smile, just grunt and snort
It makes you wonder if life is worth living.

March 4, 1986

Boredom

Boredom is around us day and night.
We can't get rid of it,
And it makes us uptight.
It curses the gloom that's set upon us.
I wish the sun would dawn around us.

April 7, 1986

HELL

Taste the fire
Feel the flames
Burn with desire
Live with the pains
Now you pay for all your sins
Roast on the stake with needles and pins.

April 25, 1986

Lightning Strikes

My Dearest:
   A Poem For you
Lightning strikes

Lightning strikes from the sky
You sweep me off my feet with your sigh
I wish to never say good bye oh bye
My living reflection of a dream.
You now seem to be a part of me,
It's like I include you in my every thought.
Thinking of you makes my blood run hot
Burning passion before I have fought
In real life I see you not
But in my dreams we've tied the knot.
   The End
Love Always, *Greg*

April 30, 1986

MY GIRLFRIEND

You're more exciting than a ten pin strike,
More beautiful than a full moon on a bright summer's
night.
I look at you and know there's clear sailing ahead,
Warm nights to clear my head,
A part of you will be with me always,
I wish to go forward and never sideways.
Read this poem and remember me well,
For I will remember you as clear as a bell.
This may rhyme and go as a chime,
But for today I know that you're mine.

May 5, 1986

POEMS OF MINE

With a pencil in my hand
And a thought in my mind
I can jot this down to go as a rhyme
From time to time it really is fine
To write these poems of mine.

May 16, 1986

Escape

Fly me higher,
For I won't tire.
I wish to see the world as a flyer.
Don't shoot me down,
For I will drown,
In the depth of the ocean,
With water abound.
Hear me cry,
Hear my sound,
I mourn for a lost love,
Buried under ground.
For the sake of beauty, for the sake of shame,
The memory I have will remain.
The soul within my aching heart
Can't tame the pain that took us apart.

June 8, 1986

Cow Shoe

There once was a cow named Moo,
Who had one very bright shoe.
He was walking one day,
In a stack full of hay,
And stepped on a needle or 2.

June 9, 1986

GONE

The moon shines upon water.
Reflections of days gone by, I see,
Memories of you Slowly
        Slowly
        Slip away into gray.
I see no one but you.
        In
        Water I see,
The moon. Coyotes, I hear, they bay at distant
Moon I see, They also see.
The Moon is gone now, covered by Black
        White
        Cloud
They bring back memories of you, Now
        Gone, Somewhere in the Past?
        Future?
        Distance?
        Gone to peacefulness Gone!

June 10, 1986

FOREVER

They seek someone to free them from the dead,
They are lost souls in a forbidden land,
Trying to be free of the wicked hand,
They are evil or so it has been said,
Victims of the demon seed,
They're the lost forgotten dead.
They want to catch a passing breeze,
To fly away over the seas,
The devil clutches them on their knees,
The devil plays with them, they have to please.
If they only knew he was all lies,
Maybe they could escape the one they despise,
But they have done wrong in some past life,
But tell me now: does anyone deserve such a punish-
ment
As hell as a final resting place?

July 10, 1986

THE LIGHT

What can I say at the end of the day,
It feels like I've been dumped into the hay?
I love her so much but needless to say,
She doesn't love me in quite the same way.
I need her to stay close to my heart,
And not to shoot through me, such as a dart.
I want to stay friends or just a little bit more,
But what she said today tore me apart.
She is my friend, which never will end,
But if I can't have her, I never will mend.
Read this well, for you never can tell
Whose mind will change with a little persuasion.
I wish she would turn her mind to the light
And see how everything could work out right.

August 6, 1986

Loves a thing thats hard to grasp
hard to hold
and hard to make last
Love to many is fresh and beutifull
Love to me is cold and brital
Love should last forever
In total honesty
to pretend to love is a sin
and a wast of time.
To love and leave is a shame
and the pain it brings is hard to tame

AUG 9

WHAT IS LOVE

Love's a thing that's hard to grasp,
Hard to hold,
And hard to make last.
Love to many is fresh and beautiful.
Love to me is cold and brittle.
Love should last forever,
In total honesty.
To pretend to love is a sin,
And a waste of time.
To love and leave is a shame,
And the pain it brings is hard to tame.

August 9, 1986

Sweet emotions
Hard destortios
Soft comotions
Bitter devotions
Snow is cold
love is cold
love to me is hard to fel
To me love can't bind
love has rendered me helpless
love has rendered me again
Time and time again
my soul acks
love ~~its, as~~ knows no shame
love isn't ~~the one~~ to blame
love consume
and it's hard to tame

Its bitter pain
is desire with no mane
~~love in thruogh can be~~
to find the love is a vilent fight
A tragek lose in the night
To find a love is afright
This would surly be a shoking sight
Maybe I might go on a life light
To find A love to last an eternity
I dout it though

Aug 23/86

Just
Started
on
Tape

Tragek
Tragek
Tragk

26   Gregory "Crash" Cooper

OH, What a Sweet Emotion

Sweet emotions
Hard distortions
Soft commotions
Bitter devotions
Snow is cold
Love is cold
Love to me is hard to find
To me surely love can't bind
Love has rendered me helpless
Time and time again
My soul aches
Love knows no shame
Love isn't to blame
Love can surely maim
And it's hard to tame
Its bitter pain is desire with no name
To find a love is a violent fight
A tragic loss in the night
To find a love is a fright
This would surely be a shocking sight
Maybe I might go on a life-long plight
To find a love to last an eternity
I doubt it though

August 23, 1986

LOVE PROGRESSES

The morning is misty with dew on the ground,
Just like a love not sure what it's found.
It hears the sound of animals awaking,
And as the day progresses love starts quaking.
It grows and grows and never slows,
And pretty soon it goes to show
It doesn't rain on every dewy day.
Unlike love, everyday must end,
And like love sometimes not with a beautiful Sunset.

September 8, 1986

The Queen of Hearts

Across the horizon, the sun sets gently into the sea,
Walking on the beach is the Queen of Hearts, and me.
Her voice, so soothing,
Her love, so tender.
The moon is rising
The devil's hate I'm despising.
He has condemned her from love,
And the dove he is hiding.
From her, I beg for forgiveness.
I have dared the forbidden,
My love for her has risen and risen.
She asks the Prince for the dove of peace
But the Prince of Darkness carries a grudge.
He's jealous of her beauty,
And quieting of pain,
But he must have his way, for he is insane.
The moon is leaving now,
Replaced by the sun,
And the devil is burning,
The dove's on the run.
The Queen of Hearts has to catch the bird of peace,
Then maybe I'll win
The love that lies deep within.

October 18, 1986

Remember

Remember walking in the sand,
So in love, hand in hand.
The sun was setting beyond the sea,
The birds were singing for you and me.
For hours and hours we walked and talked,
The waves on the sand seemed to mock.
Then we reached home,
The evening was done,
The romance and love I never will shun.
If I could walk into yester years,
I'd be there with you and not these tears.

October 22, 1986

Shelter and Misty Tears

Give me shelter,

There're misty tears falling.

My freedom has been captured,

And is a prisoner of love.

My eyes once held sadness,

Now they are dancing.

What could be more beautiful,

Than two people fitting in harmony perfectly.

Laughing,

Crying,

Lusting,

Examining each,

    Loving.

November 3, 1986

SKY BLUE

Sky blue,

Heart ache red.

Sky blue when I met you,

Heart ache red, when hate you fed.

When loving you, life was dreamy,

When breaking up with you, life got steamy.

When loving you, life had a warm red glow,

Near the end it was blue cold.

To kill my life it would mean burning red down below.

To stick it out could mean sky blue forever.

Sky blue,

Heart ache red.

Sky blue when I met you,

Heart ache red when hate you fed.

Someday I must look truth in the eye,

And ask if I really care.

If I do, then I choose you.

November 12, 1986

Paradise

As the sun set, lying to sleep in the sea,
The sky turned pink and mauve.
The moon we could see, a huge silver disk,
Coming clearer as the sun closed its restful eyes.
Long, skinny, black clouds partly covered
The moon, giving it an awesome, eerie look,
Almost voodoo.
The moon, with its hypnotic effect, almost put us to
sleep.
All we could do was look and wonder,
Until dawn opened her sleepy eyes, then
once again we are shrouded by day.

November 19, 1986

VIBRANT VIOLET

Walking through a field,
of vibrant violet flowers,
One can feel the power of silence.
It shrouds one's mind with purple haze
And one is sure to remember these days.
Although it must end, but not for awhile,
One will come back wearing a smile.
But soon it is lonely, as one usually is,
And one needs a friend and thinks two in a whiz.
Walking through a field,
of vibrant violet flowers,
Two can feel the power of love.
It fills two's, body and soul, with purple haze,
As two rejoice, never leaving these days.
But two are alone in a world that fulfills every need but
one,
Two realize and two sacrifice body, mind and soul.
As time moves on the moulding begins and
Two become one, just as it was, in a whiz.
Two now walk, acting as one,
Through fields of vibrant violet flowers.
Forever together,
Leaving paradise
Never.

December 14, 1986

QUESTIONS

Never ask questions, or you may find answers.
Then, your excuse of ignorance is shot,
No longer can you act such as a tot.

December 14, 1986

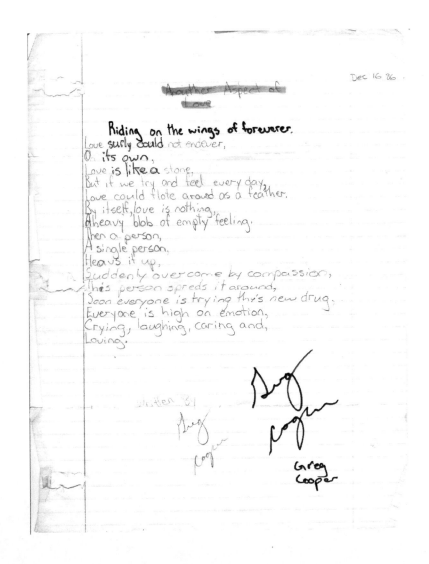

Dec 16 86

~~Another Aspect of~~
~~love~~

Riding on the wings of foreverer.
Love surly could not endever,
On its own,
Love is like a stone,
But if we try and feel every day,
Love could flote around as a feather.
By itself, love is nothing,
A heavy blob of empty feeling.
Then a person,
A single person,
Heavs it up,
Suddenly overcome by compassion,
This person spreds it around,
Soon everyone is trying this new drug,
Everyone is high on emotion,
Crying, laughing, caring and,
Loving.

Written By
Greg
Cooper

Greg
Cooper

Another Aspect of Love

   Riding on the wings of forever,
Love **surely could** not endeavour,
On **its own.**
Love **is like a** stone,
But if we try and feel everyday,
Love could float around as a feather.
By itself, love is nothing,
A heavy blob of empty feeling.
Then a person,
A single person,
Heaves it up,
Suddenly overcome by compassion,
This person spreads it around.
Soon everyone is trying this new drug,
Everyone is high on emotion,
Crying, laughing, caring and,
Loving.

December 16, 1986

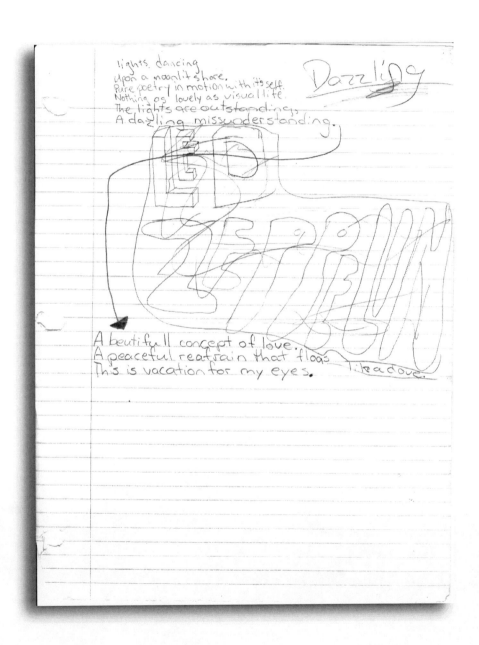

lights. dancing
Upon a moonlit shore.
Pure poetry in motion with it self.
Nothing as lovely as visual life.
The lights are outstanding,
A dazzling missunderstanding.

Dazzling

LED ZEPPLIN

A beutifull concept of love.
A peaceful reafrain that floas   like a dove
This is vacation for my eyes.

Dazzling

Lights dancing
Upon a moonlit shore.
Pure poetry in motion with itself.
Nothing as lovely as visual life.
The lights are outstanding,
A dazzling misunderstanding.
A beautiful concept of love.
A peaceful refrain that floats like a dove.
This is vacation for my eyes.

December 31, 1986

March 2 81

I am Alive   written By

~~[crossed out]~~

I spark ~~light~~ a candle,
A flicker of light,
Dim beutay to brush my eyes,
I smell a flower,
Sweet fragrance it brings,
It takes me across yellow desert streems,
I listen to doves, coo in pleasat olave trees,
Their sounds caress my ears,
This must be paridise after being dead for years.
This is how it must work,
Fore I have no better conseption
We die then live is my only preseption
When I was dying I thought I was living
Now I am living and know I was dying,
My life long ago was full of pain a sorow
We fought for the best in a world I detest
Now I am Here to build as I please,
A place to live,
Free of disease.
A place to love,
A brotherhood of kin,
The only place truly free of sin.
        I am Alive.

40   Gregory "Crash" Cooper

I am Alive

I spark a candle,
A flicker of light,
Dim beauty to brush my eyes,
I smell a flower,
Sweet fragrance it brings,
It takes me across yellow desert streams,
I listen to doves coo in pleasant olive trees,
Their sounds caress my ears,
This must be paradise after being dead for years.
This is how it must work,
For I have no better conception,
We die then live is my only perception.
When I was dying I thought I was living,
Now I am living and know I was dying.
My life long ago was full of pain, a sorrow,
We fought for the best in a world I detest.
Now I am Here to build as I please,
A place to live,
Free of disease.
A place to love,
A brotherhood of kin,
The only place truly free of sin.
   I am Alive

March 2, 1987

Trapped!

My body is a cold prison of,
Punishment and reward,
My body is a life support for my brain,
My brain holds my soul that pleads to fly.
My soul urns to get out, I feel about to explode.
This life as we know it, becomes more materialistic,
As the days drift by,
Distraction and greed we live on.
I want to fly to a world of love.
I look to the stars, and wonder,
Is such a world possible or even likely?
I want to soar between the stars and lear blissfulness,
I want to be free of mind and body,
These that scar.
I want to master emotion.
I want to escape.

Trapped

My body is a cold prison of
Punishment and reward.
My body is a life-support for my brain.
My brain holds my soul that pleads to fly.
My soul yearns to get out, I feel about to explode.
This life as we know it becomes more materialistic
As the days drift by.
Destruction and greed we live on.
I want to fly to a world of love.
I look to the stars and wonder:
Is such a world possible or even likely?
I want to soar between the stars and learn blissfulness.
I want to be free of mind and body, these that scar.
I want to master emotion.
I want to escape.

August 23, 1987

DREEAMS

Dreams are the substance of life.

They fester and grow with every sleep-filled breath.

Though we seldom remember these separate lives,

They fill us with emotion.

These dreams are quiet reminders of our pain and
happiness.

They leave us dazed or sometimes vividly refreshed.

How can one explain these phenomena of life?

They elude us.

August 23, 1987

Ohh, Baby It's Dark

It's getting so dark,

I can no longer see,

Soon a bright light is staring at me.

My body is numb,

My mind is at ease,

My soul will fly with the next passing breeze.

Ohh, baby it's dark,

An' I'm goin' away,

Ohh, baby it's dark,

I wish I could stay.

There's some ancient voice,

I cannot explain,

Some Ancient calling,

A sweet wavering refrain.

Ohh, baby it's dark,

I wish I could stay,

Ohh, baby it's dark,

An' I'm goin' away.

September 2, 1987

LIMPING CUTLERY

As I watch you gaze toward a misty moon,
I remember when we were as different as a fork to a
spoon.
Those days are gone now like a fleeting glimpse.
We are together, our love no longer limps.
With so much in common, we can no longer deny
That fighting our feelings was a useless try.

September 21, 1987

I DON'T GET IT

Did ja ever feel like blowin' up?
All the questions with no answers.
Did ja ever feel like ya wanna explode?
Com' on now, did anyone treat ya like a kid?
Com' on babe, do ya know how it bites?
What's it all for, darling?
Why does it all happen?
Answer my question!
What's the point in it all?
It's just punishment,
For what?!
It's just reward,
What the Hell for?
HUH?

Late 1987

I Wonder

I walk this road of fortune and misfortune.
I have no idea when my road will end.
I do things that mean so little to me, but
It sets others' anger free.
My road is sidelined with different people,
Occasional acquaintances that eventually turn on a
different road.
I think materialistic objects force people away
From pursuing the light or the truth,
Whatever that may be.
As I walk, sometimes, I wonder.

October 31, 1987

This Is How It Works

In the deepest, darkest realm of last thought recognition, one might wonder how echoing reflections describe one's self. A single image in eternity's dusty mirror, one speck forgotten over a never ending plane of reality. The grip of fantasy often rips one away from the ongoing plane, only to release, and one tumbles back, spinning and confused, back to the norm.

November 2, 1987

ORIGINALITY

The ideals of society in general

need not interfere with

those of the individual.

Sometime in 1987

Beyond Reason?

The desolation and non-existence, save mere acquaintance, places a heavy load on one's soul. The perplexity of mortal man almost exceeds that of the reason for life itself. The meaning of existence is purely a piece of any one man's opinion. Each to his own.

November 19, 1987

SOMEWHAT PERPLEXING?

The co-existence of

each individual is

relative to the point of

being human.

November 19, 1987

Autumn

A brilliant, vividly red leaf
Drifts downward and comes to rest
On crisp frostbitten grass.
It is Autumn,
Beautiful things become brilliant and die,
So that Spring may bring the next generation.

November 19, 1987

BAPTISM

I baptise my fears in life's murky presence,
A dire, blunt opponent,
That makes me look to death
For freedom.
Death is all but what you imagine it to be.
Some truly die.

January 3, 1988

Humanity's Problem

Humanity's problem is its materialistic dilemmas.
Look on past your colours and straight lines,
Look on past your glittery diamonds and your fast cars,
Turn toward the light and drop your wants,
Slow down, take what you need,
Learn to be happy,
Satisfaction guaranteed.

January 10, 1988

One Touch

One touch from the boundary of passion,
But one touch from all romance and fiction,
Baby, one scream to damn every bit.
Only fear and intense passion
Drive our pounding hearts to mould,
Only our quiet connecting souls make it enough
To abide years of dying.
Just touch me, once is almost enough.

January 23, 1988

MY SOUL

My soul is a latent obscurity

roaming aimlessly

in this time of dying.

January 24, 1988

The Reason, to Mingle?

Oh, why must we mingle with the dying,
While dying ourselves?
Is it to learn to live?
Or, is it simply to pass the time,
To fill one's empty spaces?
There must be a reason to mingle
Before life begins.

February 1, 1988

What If?

Sleep is a big world,
For sleep brings on great fantasies,
Or realities?
If many souls fantasize about Valhala,
Is there not such a place?
Maybe I am not in reality,
I'm in a nightmare or fantasy.
Maybe reality is much nicer.
Possibly this fantastic world
Is to keep the fantasy alive.

February 2, 1988

Ones Next Step

One must watch one's step,
For in death, the next one may be an enmesh.
One misguided foot may lead one away
From life as they may want it.

February 3, 1988

Shake Your Mind

   If you so choose
You could shake your mind.
Many things you may find.
Sanity, honesty, truth and creativity.
Shake your brain.
Look for the right way to eventually live.

February 3, 1988

Push to Prepare

Why are so many lead away from learning, in death,
To live.

Commercialism and propaganda, for many, can't be
denied.

One can't obliterate these, impossible, but one can
push,

Push them aside for awhile.

Prepare for one's life.

February 3, 1988

A Thought

The decisive mind is one with many questions.
Although an indecisive mind may not care about such
deep things
As life and death, they may despise those who critique
them as being
stupid.

February 4, 1988

Hole New Infinity

I look in my mind and a hole new
Infinity awakes.
It is empty,
I can see forever.
How in one lifetime can I fill the
Empty space?
Is there any point?
Can it be done tomorrow?

February 4, 1988

The Inter Zone

In the inter zone
Life springs vividly to life,
Suddenly, like a wheel turns to spin.
I have yet to be,
I have yet to brother one who has been.
One must meander along flat lands of boredom,
Or, one must be thrashed down mountains of reward
And punishment.
Before one is accepted to the place where souls
infinitely fly,
One must be born
With spirit and soul.

February 5, 1988

TAKE ME HIGHER

ROCK AND ROLL

      I listen to psychodalia,
Yawn, close my eyes,
And listen to the sweet fragrance,
Of Music.

February 7, 1988

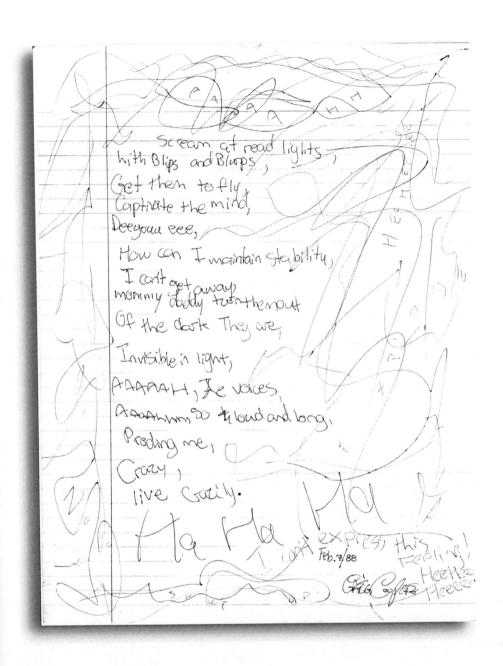

Scream at read lights,
With Blips and Blurps,
Get them to fly,
Captivate the mind,
Deeyouu eee,

How can I maintain stability,
I can't get away,
mommy daddy turn them out
Of the dark They are,

Invisible in light,
AAAAAH, the voices,
Aaaahhmm So loud and long,
Proding me,
Crazy,
live Crazily.

Ha Ha Ha

I can't express this feeling!
Feb. 7/88   Hee Hee
Greg Cooper   Heeee

AAAAHH

Scream at red lights
With Blips and Blurps.
Get them to fly,
Captivate the mind.
Deeyouu eee.
How can I maintain stability?
I can't get away,
Mommy, daddy, turn them out
Of the dark,
They are invisible in light.
AAAAAH, the voices,
AAAAAH, so loud and long.
Prodding me,
Crazy,
Live crazily.

Ha Ha Ha
I can't express this feeling!
HeeHeeHeeee

February 7, 1988

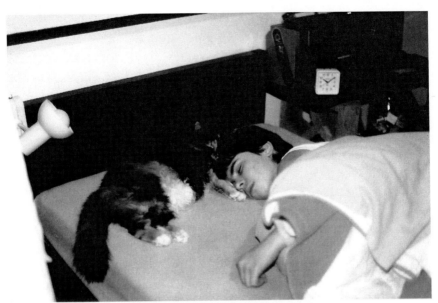

CHILLIN' WITH TIGGER AKA WIGGINS.

HAPPY 15TH 1986.

FUN IN THE SUN WITH MATT, JOHN, GREG AND ?.

DRAMA CLASS 1986 GREG AND SCOTT.

GREG'S 1ST WORKSHOP!

GREG AND PAT POPEK 1987.

PAT AND GREG, GOOD FRIENDS, 1987.

BILL, FARRELL, GREG, TODD AND PAT 1987.

LED ZEPPLIN CAKE.

GRADE 10 GRAD. 1987.

GERRY

DOUBLE TROUBLE, GREG & GERRY 1988.

1989 GREG WITH FIRST LOVE......ALEXIS.

ALEXIS & GREG, PHOTO OP. GREG'S 1989 GRAD NIGHT

GREG'S 1989 GRADUATION NIGHT FROM STEVESTON
SR. SECONDARY WITH MOM, BEV

BRACES, A RIGHT OF PASSAGE. 1988.

1989 GRAD NIGHT WITH SISTER, SHANNON

1989 GRAD NIGHT WITH DAD, STAN

THE UNION CREW WITH GREG AND JULIE, 2006.

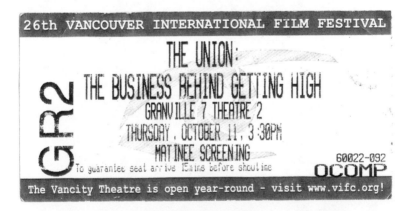

GREG STARRED IN THIS AWARD WINNING DOCUMENTARY
REGARDING MEDICAL MARIJUANA.

2012 RE: 1998 DOCUMENTARY ON THE NATURE OF THINGS.

GREG "CRASH" IN 2012.

STOP

I am exhausted from words.
I have nothing left,
No more creativity. For now,
It will be just thoughts.
For now,
It is a lull,
It shan't last,
It can't last. It can't end like a song,
I may hate it with burning detestment (sic),
But it is my obsession.
I stay sane,
I sort everything out.
Like night turns to day,
My pen turns on paper.
It must happen,
It is logical.
Just as gentle waves lap the shore,
Forever,
I will have words,
If nothing else,
I will have my soul,
Which carries these words.
Still I cannot think of anything
But my thoughts.
To write,
Is becoming my life.
It dumps out without end,

To stop it would be futile.

The same words over and over,

In different context,

And never without meaning,

The end of the page may be near,

And linger,

Threatening the end.

But sometimes to move to a clean sheet

Is healthy.

So, healthy I am.

Am I happy?

I feel like a void right now.

But my thoughts hurt.

Is it really so healthy?

Or is it dangerous?

  Stop!

February 7, 1988

Peace, Dove and Feather

Materialism goes with the modernistic snob
As pink and gray play.
Banish!
Oh them to be exiled,
The snob and materialism,
Pink and Gray to stay.
Pink and Gray complement that individual which is
concerned
With only his fellow inhabitant's well being and being
one with himself.
Pink and Gray go together like
Peace, Dove and Feather.
Complementary Beauty.
None more need be present
Save love, indeed, love.
Aahh, you may say
"But we need some materialism."
Yes! But not corrosive name brand rags,
One needs but warm skin,
The nitty gritty is to where the issue falls,
To the Roots we need go,
Tap souls for the importance of "Death".
You are becoming sister kin,
brother kin.
Learn to live I say.
Find your belief and believe it.
Hold fast your own destiny.

Learn and be wise.

    True, everything is relative,

    Until you leave.

Then love is what counts,

    If you believe.

Fantasy is accepted if only you stay in bounds

With reality. Oh, but another issue altogether.

Reality? Don't question it, it just is.

    It just is

        Peace, Dove and Feather.

Save love. Indeed love,

    And This Death,

        Are all but relative.

Should one believe in materialistic

Obsessions? are all it is.

Sure, believe and go no farther than the grave,

    Ashes sprinkled on a feather,

White, dusted upon your heart.

Do you know? Or is it a fallacy?

A deceiving lie is what it is.

    I despise it.

        It is a new Cult.

Be careful of its colourful magnetism.

It can drain you of spirit

Oh No Not your soul.

    Where will you go without that?

What makes you dimensional?

    A diamond is what you become,

A clear rock mounted on the gold band of society.

Oh frightful society,
A huge farce
That prods the pity of masses.
Shameful Shameful all you diamonds
That make society a big machine.
The colours matter not. It just is
Peace, Dove and Feathers.
Save love. Indeed, love
And this death.
Please, In death learn to live. It's
all it's supposed to mean.

February 9, 1988

TIGGER, MY BEST FRIEND - SHE
ALWAYS KNEW BEST. 1974-1987

Can Ya feel it?

Can ya feel it?
Can ya feel the feeling?
Electric butterflies,
Making me unstable.
The feeling,
It lies between us,
When I look you in the eyes.
When I look you in the eyes,
You are, pure beauty,
Not to be denied.
Can ya feel it?
Sweet thunder rumbling inside,
Inside you, inside me.
Like the flash of lightning
Sweet thunder,
We both share.
You are my comet,
My Queen of hearts,
It feels right in my soul.
Can ya feel it?
Intense Euphoria on a cool winters night.
Can ya feel it?
It lies between us,
Be my girl,
be mine,
If just for awhile,
Be with me.
Can ya feel it?

Feb. 12/88

45

Can Ya Feel It?

Can ya feel it?
Can ya feel the feeling?
Electric butterflies
Making me unstable.
The feeling,
It lies between us,
When I look you in the eyes.
You are, pure beauty,
Not to be denied.
Can ya feel it?
Sweet thunder rumbling inside,
Inside you, inside me,
Like the flash of lightning,
Sweet thunder,
We both share.
You are my comet,
My Queen of Hearts.
It feels right in my soul.
Can ya feel it?
Intense Euphoria on a cool winter's night.
Can ya feel it?
It lies between us.
Be my girl,
Be mine,
If just for awhile,
Be with me.
Can ya feel it?

February 12, 1988

The Expiation of a Timeless Curse

No more deep shall darken my shadow eyes.
No more shallow may cast deception upon my charac-
ter.
A pleasant song, reminder of sin,
Wallows amongst the dark side of comprehension.
The pain will stay as a lesson ill forgot.
Lest we forget the chosen.
Her beauty, too rich for consumption, must fester in
admiring hearts,
Lest we forget the forgotten.
And so grows the song.
The song. And exists the knowing,
I have not lost, nor shall I ever.

June 9,1988

THE VERDICT

From below the depth of reason and
style on a plain beyond our own,
One must linger from judgment drowned
on reason of a stolen soul.
The verdict made by Lord Destitution was one
of unequalled unfairness.

Sometime in early-mid 1988

Testimony

This is my testimony,
Echoing through centuries old.
Like a sledge hammer, it's meaning crashes through.
My death is my life, my life is my death
Others have shared this for centuries old,
And will for th future past.
I can live with others,
   Though they have a different testimony,
Why can't others do the same?
I suppose it is meant to be this way.
"Everything is happening as it should,
   there are no accidents and no mistakes."
So true, it cannot exist any other way.
Hold your belief true to your heart,
Don't kill if someone ells hold anouther
Shore or not, you can still hang out.
This is my testimony.

July 22/1988

I'm a poet
I'm a philosifer,
Can't spell worth shitt though!

Testimony

This is my testimony,
Echoing through centuries old.
Like a sledge hammer, its meaning crashes through.
My death is my life, my life is my death,
Others have shared this for centuries old,
And will for the future past.
I can live with others,
     Though they have a different testimony.
Why can't others do the same?
I suppose it is meant to be this way.
"Everything is happening as it should,
There are no accidents and no mistakes."
So true, it cannot exist any other way.
Mold your belief true to your heart,
Don't kill if someone else holds another.
Share or not, you can still hang out.
This is my testimony.

July 22, 1988

Just the ~~Roblings~~ Ramblings

Just the ramblings of a teenage lunatic
Making sence or not, ramblings just the same.
So you see, you can read and scoff,
So you see, you can read and **critique**,
So you see, ya can read and weep,
So ya see, you can read and ~~belive~~, believe
Or ya see, ya can read and derive pleasure
All the same, just ~~rate~~ rambling of a
Deranged teenage lunatic.
Ya see just ramblings,
But like it or not,
You were ~~effected~~ ~~more~~ cause you read it,
To intrigued

Press Return
and indent ten
spaces and use
capitals   → The End! Ha!

July 22/1988

Just the Ramblings

Just the ramblings of a teenage lunatic
Making sense or not, ramblings just the same.
So you see, you can read and scoff,
So you see, you can read and critique,
So you see, you can read and weep,
So you see, you can read and believe,
Or you see, you can read and derive pleasure.
All the same, just ramblings of a
Deranged teenage lunatic.
You see just ramblings,
But like it or not,
You were intrigued 'cause you read it
To,
     THE END! Ha!

July 22, 1988

The Pains of Happiness

Troubled times brought me down,
For far too long I've been alone,
Alone, far too long.
I'm once again feeling the Pains of Happiness.
My honey came along, old troubles gone.
The pains of happiness drive me so fuckin' insane,
But that's the price of happiness.
I sometimes wonder if it's all going to shit.
Then my honey smiles.
The pains of happiness drive me so fuckin' insane
But then it's like my honey's smile,
Everything seems to fit.
Like the vast blue sea, my honey and me,
So much to explore, so much emptiness
Like the pains of happiness.

August 17, 1988

The Sweetness of the Thunder

The sweetness of the Thunder,
Such is the feeling,
The sweetness of the Thunder,
The thought of eternal ecstasy.
The sweetness of the Thunder,
Such is the feeling,
The flash of her smile,
The sweetness of the Thunder,
Like the rush of a kiss,
The kiss I miss,
The kiss **I miss,**
The rush inside,
Like the speed of Thunder,
Such is the feeling
Of the kiss I miss.
My Davina,
My Vina,
Her name so devine,
The glimpse of lightning,
The Thunder in the sky,
The sweet rush of the Thunder,
My Davina devine.

August 18, 1988

A Dangerous Moment

A dangerous moment,
A brush with flesh,
The flash of a blade,
The moment called death.
A dangerous moment,
Not to be denied,
A feeling of helplessness,
A feeling inside.
The slyness of the quarry,
The fear of the prey,
The love of the game
By all who play.
The trip is over,
The moment of truth,
Intense paranoia,
The decision
To Live or Die.

August 18, 1988

The Ultimate Love

You are my comet, shot across the sky
with fire and passion.

I tremble at your glance, I am
suspended in this trance.

You are a polished diamond amongst stones,
colourless and insignificant.

You are my warmth, existing in my
heart and soul.

Intense desire to hold you, I want to
laugh and dance with you.

My mind is delirious with your presence,
you are intoxicating.

You are pure poetry in motion,
to be compared with nothing, you are above all.

I want to fly with you,
over the clouds and into the sun.

The sun is less blinding than your radiance,
your eyes sparkle with life.

The magic you possess is potent,
you have cast a spell and I have caught it.

Not enough can be said, there are
too many emotions.

I shall have you, if not for a moment
then never.

October 2, 1988

DEPARTURE

I bare with me the love
and fears of hopeful tears.
The caring hearts of yesterday,
now my boat sails away.

October 1988

RAGE

    All at once I am shattered,
with not a thing to look forward to,
    Once again I ask myself "what's it all for?"
and once again there are no answers.
    In my silent rage,
I can only wait for the revolution to pause at
some happy time, sometime.
    I have thought to end this torturing existence,
but that is not right, something says it's not right.
    Something in this empty rage says keep going.
    Going on and on and on,
I get tired, where am I going in life?
    Just drifting, I guess, till it's over.
    It's over and now I Fly??

November 25, 1988

XMAS

How dazzling are the lights,
like the shine of moon lit icicles
dangling from snow dusted branches.
Christmas is mumbled
under the breath of all,
Of all Jesus is responsible
for the love and warmth of caring hearts.
Like the lights,
so are our eyes at the sight
of snow drifting carelessly to the ground.
And like Jesus's,
our dreams hopefully fulfilled.

Like the twilight glow
on snow capped mountains
Children young and old,
rejoice, with starry eyes,
At the Dawn
of yet another wondrous Season.
Such is the glow,
of children young and old,
That sparks the yuletide
flame and sets alight the warmth of Christmas.

December 1988

WAITING

If love is the essence of life,
Then what is the essence of love?
   You are the essence of my love, eternally,
Yet you are blocked by materialism,
One might say, inexperience,
I might agree,
Then wait.

December 8, 1988

Oh Painful Youth

Oh, painful youth,
The treachery of childhood,
To face the facts,
To learn the lessons,
To understand reality.
   Oh, painful youth,
Go forth with unsuspecting eyes,
Go forth and be taught
By common foe,
Go forth to yonder world, its open arms await.
   Oh, painful youth,
To exist but for a fleeting moment,
To wield its rusty sword
Only for a time,
To forbid childhood forever more.
   Oh, painful youth,
How I detest ye,
Yet I know only this present plight,
How I love ye
For some buried forever, lost reason,
How I am tested time and time again.
   Oh, painful youth.

December 8, 1988

I Follow You

I follow you,
In Reality then Dreams,
Across the sky,
Across the sea.
I follow you,
Forever however far
Over the moon,
Over the stars.
I follow you,
My Beauty,
My every Breath.
I follow you
Your Grace,
Your magic.
I follow you
To eternity and back.

To continue in Harmony,
To weave our emotional tapestry,
I follow you.
You've stolen my heart.
You've lit my stars.
(Look at) Your midnight eyes,
(Catch) Your misty glance,
I follow you.
You have restored colour to my dreams

And I am thankful for all,
    I'll follow you.
You have blown my mind,
You have taken my hand,
    I'll follow you.
For I am the chosen,
For me (there was) no choice.
    I follow you to eternity and back.

January 8, 1989

My Obsession

You are my obsession
My glory,
My life's eternal song.
Your long dark hair
Fuels my passion
That burns for nights so long.
To have you,
To hold you,
Would make me complete.
To know you,
To love you,
I dream in my sleep.
You are the one,
And the only,
For me to have close.
You are the one I adore
You mean the most.

January 9, 1989

*Mr. Boffo (Gerry) needed a poem for a special
girl. So I wrote this, he never used it.*

Dedicated To Her Song

Evening Stars glisten in her eyes
She is one with the universe.
My every moment is dedicated to her song
~~My every bout but I feel it all~~
My every Thought prolongs her ~~image~~
My destiny is with her,
My pounding heart beats to her name,
One moment in time with her,
And I shall know what love is.
For I have shun all others, ~~and~~ I am dedicated
to her ~~song~~
Eternaly.   Jan.10/89   Greg Cooper.

Dedicated to Her Song

Evening stars glisten in her eyes.
She is one with the universe.
My every moment is dedicated to her song.
My every thought prolongs her image.
My destiny is with her,
My pounding heart beats to her name.
One moment in time with her
And I shall know what love is.
For I have shunned all others.
I am dedicated to her song,
Eternally.

January 10, 1989

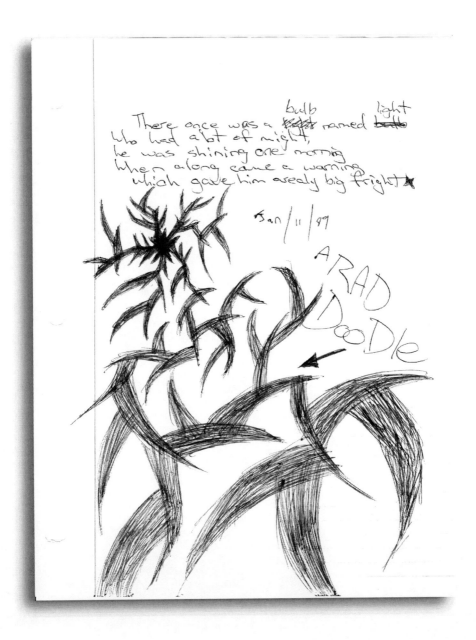

There once was a ~~bulb~~ named ~~light~~
Who had a lot of might,
he was shining one morning
When along came a warning
Which gave him a realy big fright ★

Jan/11/99

A RAD
DOODLE

SHINING

There once was a bulb named light
Who had a bit of might.
He was shining one morning
When along came a warning
Which gave him a really big fright.

January 11, 1989

Everything to You

Sweeter than wine, fruit of the vine,
Just hold onto me, continue to shine.
On the wings of forever, we shall endeavour
To our destiny, eternity, we'll drift on a feather.
Enticing is your scream, on the wind like a dream.
Everything to you or have you seen
A single tear, kills me, my dear.
You are all emotions, your beauty runs deep
The day is too short, why must we sleep?
To you I give all, mind, body and soul.
Everything to you, for you I would fall.
Sweet is the thunder that roars in my soul,
Gone is the emptiness, filled is the hole.
For you, to me, are the only one,
Everything to you, now it is done.

January 26, 1989

In the Back of My Mind

Alone last night, in a dreamy state,
Somewhere in the back of my mind,
The winds of thought arose and became a storm.
Alone last night, in a dark dreamy state,
Somewhere deep in the back of my mind,
The storm became a thunderous, horrific hurricane.
Sometimes, alone, in the back of my mind,
It rains rage,
When the levee breaks, I'll have no place to go.

February 5, 1989

Greg's note: 'When the Levee Breaks' — Led Zeppelin

> *"and don't it make ya feel bad
> when you're tryin' to find your
> way, Oh, ya don't know which way
> to go."*

Don't Take Me From My Cloud

It's more than you know,
Leave me alone,
Go somewhere else.
  Don't upset the things that are different,
You're not the same as me,
You're a downer,
Really insecure.
  If you don't like me,
Take off,
Don't provoke me,
I'm liable to explode on you.
  Just blow away,
Don't talk to me,
Leave me in peace,
With my friends,
They know or they wouldn't be with me.
  I can dance and sing,
Can you?
  You cut people down to the ground,
You're jealous,
Don't cut me or my friends down,
Don't take me from my cloud,
I'm having fun and trippin' out,
Just on being.
  Don't take me from my cloud,
It's a waste of your time and mine,
And it really doesn't make you feel any better,

And I feel like shit.

    If you think ill of me,

Don't make it my problem.

    Don't take me from my cloud,

We're both different,

You and me,

That's not bad,

It's reality.

    Just work with me,

We can all get along,

If you're not going to try,

Then leave me alone,

But just

    Don't take me from my cloud.

February 6, 1989

IN MY BUBBLE, BEHIND MY WALL

In my bubble, behind my wall,
I am secluded and nothing can touch me.
In my bubble, behind my wall,
My soul turns cold and I can feel no emotion.
I am lonely sometimes,
In my bubble behind my wall.
I am safe from things that may scar my character,
In my bubble behind my wall.
I do come out, if only for awhile,
To reveal myself, but I am vulnerable, that cannot be.
So I sit here,
In my bubble behind my wall, and watch the world go by.

March 1, 1989

STAGES

Anxious void, rage or depression

desire to let it out

desire to write

find the words

scribble them down

think about what is written

relate it to myself

Then, I am somewhat at ease.

March 1, 1989

This Stranger of Mine

The Stranger is a mystery to me,
The Stranger is my power and my strength,
The Strangeness of this feeling,
The bizarre tangle of fright, nervousness and love.
Who is this Stranger of mine?
She moves me and I think nothing of myself,
And I am moved in a strange way.
Fleeting intensity in my heart,
And my soul feels life and it is good.
I will let this feeling blossom,
As flowers drenched in the love of sunshine.
And this Stranger of mine will come to me,
And we shall grow, we shall feel life,
For how it is meant to feel, and it is good.
Why has this Stranger chosen me?
Why have I chosen this Stranger?
The speed is too harsh,
I can't slow down,
To touch you is a rush and you have touched me,
My senses tingle at a glance and you have touched me
Deep in the spasms of my thoughts,
I can think of nothing but the Strangeness of
This feeling.
Alexis, you are my Stranger and I feel strength,
Pulsating from the Strangeness of love and it
Echoes between you and I.
What's it like inside? Open up and let

Me know you, let me see the lights in your eyes,

And you will know as I know,

And you are my Stranger.

March 13, 1989

Lavender Eyes

All at once, for one solid but fleeting
Glance, I saw for myself a blooming Romance.
 How could I resist, the Glance did persist,
My eyes did behold a vision so bold.
 So pretty my darling, paint me a picture
With lavender eyes and a vibrant sunset.
 Tell me a story, the setting with love,
A common cliché pure like the dove.
 Pronounce to me a syllable that
I may think up the word,
But suggest to me nothing that I have already heard.
 Then dig me a hole in the mist of my mind
To creatively fill with the past left behind.
 Like a marble that sparkles,
It sure does look good,
You are my sweety, that sounds absurd.
 Pick up your heart from where you left off,
It doesn't make sense, he said with a cough.
 Look at yourself, see what you see
Fairly appealing, now look at me.
 Daintily speaking, you are seeming blue,
So flutter by me, I'll shelter you.
 Can you hear what I say,
This might take all day
But if you open up you'll see infinity, eternity.
 What a concept, "till the end of time";
My watch has stopped, therefore have I?

Now back to my rhyming with skill so intent,
Let it all out but the meaning seems bent.
    Read it all over, try to make sense,
Study it hard, it dies in the end.
    But "now back to you", my chill so devine,
You light up my life, yet another rhyme.

Hey, I gotta go, my pen's running out
What does that mean?
I began with a shout!
Don't stop painting, lavender eyes,
And stories with settings of love are hard to come by,
But clichés with doves sure ain't!

July 12, 1989

SMILES

Once a smile has been released,
A certain light fills the sky,
    A certain sadness then is ceased,
A knowing wink of the eye.

September 1989

The Death of a Secret

The Bizarreness and injustice of
the Spectacle,
Crazily profound and almost
Reasonable, the bullet
Shot forth.
BANG!
It found its mark in her back and my heart.
To a different setting,
And therefore dressed for the occasion
I carried Her
Down the path,
Wooded on either side by a single row of Birch
And very sunny.
I take her off the path to the
Great Willow,
Giant and blooming,
Where the loving sun
Filters through the trees
Onto the green green grass,
Creating a new snowfall of
Light on the ground.
I lay her in a
Silly offerance to the
Sun.
I offer my truths and
Soul and
Secrets and

Love,
The things that escaped my mouth when
She was alive.
And I weep.

Sorrow for
Her and I.
She lost her life and I
The life I could not have with
Her. (Dead or . . .)
The sun cares and
Caresses its tenderness
On my sorrow.
Perhaps she
Flies freely
And in
Bliss, now,
Perhaps she knows how
I love her,
Deeply and sincerely.
I leave her now,
In her warm placid resting place where I know
She'll be at peace.
I hope blindly she will
Wait for me and know
That I must leave her now.
Her silky dark hair,
Her voluptuous lips,
Her tender hands.
She will wait in this

Heavenly place,
Warm and content, and
Wait for me.

October 2, 1989

LOVE HAUNTS

Love haunts the Romantic heart,
Love burns for the cool skin,
Love haunts the lonely eyes,
Love caresses the tender soul.
    In a classical melody
Love haunts.
Lovely hearts meant to be as one.
Love cares for you and yours.
In love,
A haunting stare.
In love and in despair.
My love
Forever more.
My love
Say no more.
Love haunts.

Friday October 13, 1989

Greg's note: was with Alexis in her room
when I wrote this. I love her.

Youth

A fantasy life roaring into reality,

A time of growing, learning, hurting.

A blink of the eye and it's over.

A rush of living, then maturity,

A moment of irresponsibility and lust,

An hour of emotional upheaval,

A painful time of confusion,

A wonderful time of beauty,

An age of questions,

An eon of finding the answers.

A fleeting glimps of intensity,

A slow voyage of transition,

Awhile of immortality

An end to childhood.

A devastating existence,

A smile to life,

A forever lasting friendship is made,

And true love is first experienced.

A beginning and an end,

A childhood,

A youth,

A question.

November 2, 1989

BALANCE

Aura blue horses,
Race toward a frazzling orange,
Unsuspecting sun.
To claim their loss,
And rise or fall.
Pin needled blackness,
Or,
Feather dusted white,
And thou shall emit no evil
And thou shall emit no evil.
And thou shall not shout!
Take on the wings of forever
And learn from your debts.
Smiles decrease on the ebony scale,
Smiles increase on the ivory scale.

November 12, 1989

My Angelic Moon

In a clear dream on a foggy night,
On my way to the moon,
I dreamt of my eclipsed lover.
I awake Blue and Raining,
She'll shine for me soon.
Her soul offered the invitation, Angelic,
Her smile is of the moon, full.
The attraction is the warm starry night sky,
Our love was of the warming summer breeze.
I shiver as I recall a regretful chill,
My Angelic Moon slips into her cold protective cloud,
Is seen no more and I bounce from thought
To thought, to think of her Angelic Smile.
My Angelic Moon, I miss her,
She brightens my night sky,
Mystery in her shyness,
My Angelic Moon, My Love.

November 14, 1989

Greg's note: to Alexis Ruth Hill, my first love, now lost.

Under the Sunshine

Cold reality burning the symptoms of my desire,
Like a hot hack on my frozen bloody resolve.
Tone down the colour of my unrelenting persuasion,
Painful regret in its utmost,
Drowning my reason to reason,
It is the season of my intolerable passion
To the offers of life.
    And life offers now not what I want,
And not what I cannot have,
But instead I dwell on my restrained need
And to admit I have lost is a loss.
    Under the sunshine of a proclaimed love,
I have dues and must prove my enduring compassion,
And until death I have not lost.

November 15, 1989

*Greg's note: about Alexis and I and
how I lost her to Jason. (Idiot)*

She Is Beauty In Turmoil

The gentle blush of the summer sky
Is as the quieting smile on her rosy face.
   She now has become the sky, setting mauve and
stormy
And out of my grasp.
   I am like a waterfall, crashes to its doom
And clumsily carries on.
   I am lost in my own world, a world now strange and
futile.
Like a lost soul, I walk without meaning.
   She is beauty in turmoil, a smashing wave struck on
a rocky beach.
She is distant and I watch like a gazing romantic in the
rain.
   I am caught in that turmoil,
And like an idiot I ride the next wave to the rocks.
   She is swept away by a cold breeze.
As soon as she smashes
   She is gone. I am alone
Like a tragic loss, and time marches on.
   "And so goes the song",
   I love Her.

November 16, 1989

Greg's note: again Alexis, you rule my world

I Love You

I LOVE HER MORE THAN A SHIMMERING TEAR OF JOY
LOST IN HER HOUSE OF MIRRORS
TRYING TO FIND THE TRUTH.
TOO MANY REFLECTIONS OF DAYS GONE BY
A HAZY GLANCE AT THE SKY, THE ENDLESS STARS.
IF I CHOOSE THE RIGHT GLIMMER
MAY I AGAIN GAZE INTO YOUR GLASS LIKE EYES
AND GENTLY WHISPER "I LOVE YOU" IN YOUR EAR?
YOU ARE AS OUR SHINING EARTH,
SO MUCH LIFE, SO MUCH BEAUTY, SO MUCH TO GIVE.
LET ME AGAIN SWIM YOUR OCEANS,
I LOVE THE MYSTERIES IN YOUR SKY.
HOPE IS A FLAME I BURN IN THE NIGHT TIME,
I HOPE YOU SEE THE LIGHT,
AND WITH OPEN ARMS COME TO MY COLOURLESS
WORLD.
YOU ARE AS MY DREAMS, ALL WONDERFUL THINGS.
THE ONLY WORDS THAT I WANT TO SAY,
THE ONLY CARE I WANT TO GIVE,
THE ONLY IMAGE IN MY EYES,
THE ONLY THOUGHT IN MY MIND:
YOU, I LOVE YOU.

November 22, 1989

Greg's note: Alexis, just more words

Sketches

   SOFT COLOUR SKETCHES PAINTING OUR LIVES ON
LOVE'S CANVAS,
WARM WATERS GENTLY STROKED ON YOUR CHEEKS,
HARSH OIL EMOTIONS DRIP FROM YOUR EYES,
   STORMY GRAY SKETCHES CARVING OUR LIVES ON
LOVE'S STONE.
COLD STEEL PAINFULLY CHIPS ON YOUR HEART,
CHANGING ITS LOVE MELODY
FROM ANTHEM TO CHAOS,
AND WARM WATERS TURN TORRENT AND COLD.
   AND MY LOVE LINGERS,
   AND YOUR LOVE WASHED AWAY,
   AND CHAOS' ANTHEM
DROWNS OUT MY MELODY.
   AND NOW I SKETCH WITH EMPTINESS.

November 22, 1989

Greg's note: once more Alexis, I love you.

There's a Poetic Verse in a Gold Frame

There's a verse in a gold frame on my wall,
Long aged and wrinkled paper with exquisitely pre-
served black script.
It hangs like a first love, something so honest, some-
thing never to forget.
There's a poetic verse in a gold frame on my wall,
It tells of virtue like that gained in living, sometimes
living a thousand experiences.
I read it every night, every night it glows, telling me
something true of life.
There's a poetic verse in a gold flame on my wall,
It tells of the truth but, like love, none of the rules,
sometimes I feel it burns.
There's a golden verse in a poetic flame on my wall
There's a golden verse in a poetic flame on my wall
Words truthful to truthful life
Words useless to useless life
There hangs my poetic verse in its golden frame on
my wall
And my wall hangs in my mind
And in my mind plays the music of many a poetic verse
And many a poetic verse plays on my mind.
And I still love my poetic flame that burns in the night.
And I still love my golden verse that glows in the night.
But will it ever be of any use?
Will it ever get so heavy it crumbles my wall?
And I wonder when I read my verse if it is true.

I have a poetic verse in a gold frame
I have a golden verse in a poetic flame
But she just won't see the light
And my poetic flame
Will never flicker.

November 26, 1989

Blush

Blush at me
Sing for me
Dance for me
Blush at my thought
One time
One short time
Our time.
Time never ends
Time pounds on through the lives of many
And sees many
And has seen us.
Gently Blush into my eyes
And your eyes glimmer
Our eyes meet and our eyes explode into destiny
Love never ends
And nobody lives as long as time
Time lives on and on
The sky lives on and on
Your Blush is the sky
And the sky sets mauve
Bursting again into the colours of our lives.
Everything is the rain
The rain drenches
The rain destroys
The rain comforts
And your Blush is washed away
Like a tear washes away sorrow

The rain washes everything away.
The memory of her Blush.

December 3, 1989

A Sigh's Silence

Standing beside the fullness of the feeling
of emptyness,
Laying down to sleep one more tear of
a torn heart.
Wishing to the last star of attempt
and praying it was strong enough,
And the faintness of its glimmer
causes ~~immense~~ strain, trying to see the light.

Hope is emptyness ~~yearning~~ to be filled,
but there is repried in her sigh,
And these sighs turn to screams to
silence and silence is her reprise,

Dec. 25/89

Alexis

But when one loves the
other, ~~she can't~~
one can't help

break the silence,
even if its ones last
breath.

A Sigh's Silence

Standing beside the fullness of the feeling
of emptiness,
Lying down to sleep one more tear of
a torn heart,
Wishing to the last star of attempt
and praying it was strong enough,
And the faintness of its glimmer
causes immense strain trying to see the light.
Hope is emptiness yearning to be filled,
but there is reprisal in her sigh,
And these sighs turn to screams to
silence and silence is her reprise,
But when one loves the other, one can't help
break the silence, even if it's ones last breath.

December 25, 1989

A Couple of Comparisons

    And into the twilight glow
And a lost love lives
And is distant but still beautiful like aurora borealis.
Love is eluding, glorious, unpredictable.
Loving is like navigating life by northern lights,
It is a fantasy, real, yet unreal.
    The snow is falling
Can she hear me calling?
Gazing to the sky for guidance
But through the clouds there are no lights
To lead me to her heart.
And like an abstract splattering of many a colour on
canvas
So is the abstract splattering of emotion on my mind,
And like the snow that is falling,
Such is her beauty and coldness.
And as long as I see lights in the northern sky,
There is a ray of hope to her heart.

December 30, 1989

CHEATED AND SWAYED

And as the music bursts into song
The realization that the conquest not done
Was when, at her request,
My resolve was put to the test.
An unruly consequence
Gave away to emptiness.
A pretty picture is all that remains
And sane not simple are all my pains,
Like an orchestra,
Huge but organized,
And as an overplayed tune is filed away,
So is my pain to be played on another day.
Soon to end this consequence would be nice,
But it's like rolling the dice
I feel chance will have its way
And as long as the dice are played
Chance can be cheated and swayed.

December 30, 1989

Sky Lights

Gently the sky lights
Softly dance and sketch colour across the night
And as they peek I am reminded of her blush
And will see the same sky lights in her eyes again
Come the dawn.

December 30, 1989

Country Lights

Drawn by horses down a quiet country road
The night time snow has a greenish tint
Drawn by horses in a sled on the snow
The country road vanishes into the dark behind.

Looking backward and up to the north and stretched
across the sky
The dancing sky and vanishing road paint a picture of
subtle content in my mind.

Aurora borealis slips unassuming through the dark
like a secret
Its greenish tint is a calming smile providing me with
happy memories.

After an hour or so my need was satisfied, my desire
full.
Dawn is becoming restless, rising under a warm
Chinook.

With a snap and a click, on command the team pulls
Starts me again down the lonely country road
A moving horizon, faintly dancing green, and a
warm breeze
Just one memory, a moment forever seen.

December 31, 1989

The Cause of the Swoon

Clear delusions
The way the mind works
Wavering illusions
The way the clock jerks
More confusions
The way the relationship perks
Intense intrusions
The way that life flirts
Love is the cause of the swoon.

January 1, 1990

Alexis

I hate it when it howls
In the grasping jowls of my mind,
When love is blowing around out of reach
On the shabby road of us each,
The windstorm throwing my mind in loops
Through the never ending assort-
ment of feeling's coups.

January 1, 1990

Romantic Chance

Pretty possession
Roses and ribbons
Loving relations
For granted taken not
Whirlwinds
Creating patterns plot
And never ceasing
Desires dance
Just a glance
To a romantic chance
And groping hoping
To something right
To this strange angelic moon
Lighting my night.

January 1, 1990

PRESUMPTUOUS

In your eyes there is poison,
Towards shallowness there is escape,
    Your eyes do tell all,
Easily read is what you don't say,
    And I know your every thought
But what you think you know is not right.
    Soon, though complete we will be
Because after your confusion,
Though it may not seem to be,
    Realize you will,
Your destiny's with me.
    I have your soul.

January 1, 1990

PEOPLE ARE PREDICTABLE

In order to learn how the mind works one must experiment, study, and at all times be thinking of real experiences. Experiment refers to trying new activities, hassle with people and use new words. Study, what I mean there is study your own mind firstly and secondly study other people's body language and what they say, look for contradictions, and, learn what their motives are for everything.

People are predictable.

January 2, 1990

Train of Romance

Riding this running train of romance
Surging forward at love's speed,
When I look at you my heart becomes the wheels on the
track,
Pulsating with a clickity clack.
We've bought our tickets to forever and always,
We are destined for destiny
On this running train of romance.

January 4, 1990

GIVE ME STRENGTH

Oh God
Oh merciful God
Give me strength
To let her go,
Give me the strength
And make me know.

January 6, 1990

No More Does Hope

No more does hope play a part
No more does hope ease my torn heart
I'll try not to start away regretful, hateful
I'll try not to start away forgetful.

January 6, 1990

The Candle

The candle is a symbol of happy times and sad
It's a decoration for hope
It provides both warmth and light.

January 6, 1990

To Alexis, I love you

Crowded confusion remnants
Love is like time
Give and take
Give more than take
And time you will make
Crowded confusion
Flying through time
But no closer to love
As long as you take.
Remnants and memories are all that remain
The more you give
Brighter burns the flame
And time has no meaning
To give means to love
Expect nothing in return
Just look forward to the things you deserve
And accept them
And the flame will always be in the window
I need to take nothing
I give because I love
I act out of love.

To Alexis

I love you.

January 7, 1990

HIGH

Smoky feelings,
Clear like crystal
   In a smoky room it's mystical.

January 7, 1990

ALEXIS

I will match you,
Frown for frown,
Smile for smile,
I will etch my love so deep into your heart
That by the end of time
You will know that I am the only one for you
And you will not take me for granted any longer.
I love you and I am patient.
Alexis, you were my power and my glory,
And I swear by merciful god, I love you.

January 10,1990

LOGIC

As a rule, I, take nothing for granted,
And respect is given to those so .

January 12, 1990

HONESTY

Like pretty balloons,
People are inflated with hot air,
Full of dark secrets.

January 12, 1990

It's Ironic, But It's True

Your flesh is warm, but your blood is cold,
You smile, but it's fake.
Your voice is sincere, but your words are lies,
You laugh, but it's empty,
You walk with an attitude, but that's because you're
confused,
You've etched your name in my heart, but your love
was deceiving,
You've given beauty a new name, but you're ugly
inside,
I let you go, but that's so you could blossom,
You took revenge, but that's because you're vindictive,
You'll wish to come back, but that's because you still
love me,
I still and always will love you, but that's the irony.
You will want to come back because you know I'm the
only one that really cares,

I wish I'd never seen your face, but that's because you hurt me,
You are a bitch, but that's your nature,
You're mad at me, but that's because you can't handle criticism or rejection.
I hope you grow up, because we were good together,
You're very nice, but only if you have your way.
I'd take you back, but you're stuck in your ways,
We could talk about it, but I don't have anything more to say, I've done all I can,
We could be friends, but you've forsaken me, again,
We could have been the best, but that was up to you,
We could be again, but that is up to you.
As for now it's over, but I'm willing to try, someday,
Chow baby.

January 12, 1990

TRUTH

Dungeons of shyness,
Have our insecurities locked up inside.

January 12, 1990

OBLIGATION

We are all obliged to meet our inevitable destinies,
because we must accept and live by the decisions we
make,
to ignore these outcomes would prove to be an uncom-
promising dilemma.
Open mindedness, love, caring and honesty are alter-
natives
to the gates we put up to protect the
damning evils in our minds.

January 12, 1990

TO BE YOUNG

The young people,
The precious children,
Are forced to conform to this hectic society
Without knowing beforehand the reality of unreal
pursuits,
And learn for themselves,
If they be so blessed,
That the only real things aren't objects,
But rather emotion and nature.

January 12, 1990

OPPORTUNITIES

The neon lights,

And the lamps lining the streets,

Reflect off the rainy road,

An abstract pattern of subtle colours

That disappear under the turning wheels,

Like how our desires reflect in our eyes,

They are obviously there but not so easy to figure,

And are gone with but a blink,

Like those unimportant events that add colour to my
life,

And vanish under the decisions I make.

January 12, 1990

IT'S OBVIOUS

Anything can be used for a simile or a metaphor.
Think about that and learn to learn from it.

January 12, 1990

EXPERIENCE

The weeds of my youth
Are developing my character
And are blooming through my adolescence
To become the flowers of my eventual adulthood.

January 14, 1990

If I Had a Gun

If I had a gun
And the clouds were dark
And emotion was locked in the dungeon of an attitude,
Blood and flesh would fall like rain.
But times have changed since then,
Respect isn't taken, it's earned.
If I had a gun
Remorse would sink away into bone with every deserv-
ing bullet,
And I'd ride the spasms of my mind like a horse
And my horse would show me the way.
Not necessarily to be evil but for survival,
And I'd smile only at irony and sarcasm,
If I had a gun.
If I had a gun,
A friend at my side,
A trigger of release, reprisal in a twitch
And the sunset I ride away into isn't satisfaction.
Slinging my vengeance, and so folds over another
burden
And my guilt passes with every cold breeze.
If I had a gun.
If I had a gun at my side.

January 16, 1990

APES

Living in the flesh
Exploding with one desire
Prodding in the nest
Lighting the morbid fire
Obsession in possession
Possession in obsession
A night of running sweat
Buying from concession
A sin that leaves a debt

January 17, 1990

Is Sanctuary Is Freedom

Nurturing,
The blessed rain, cooling
Grace of wind, unsettling
Blanket of cloud, warming
Thank the sun, for life
Worship blue skies, and
Curse the storm,
Refuse emotional pain,
Turn emotion into fire, and
Gaze into the flame,
Sit and wonder at the thunder,
Lightning is a silent rage,
Sanctuary is someone to hold in flowery fields,
freedom
Is sanctuary is freedom.

January 18, 1990

BE'IN BLUNT

And in the deepest sincerity
A feather is carried on the wind
And the wind whispers your name
As if my lips were on your soul
And you still breathe loneliness
A dull and cloudy sky, the rains fall
And the rains are my tears

January 20,1990

And Now I'm Gone

So, here I am, standing all alone
Remembering when it was good
You went that way and I this way
Now I'm gone,
How you shone
I thought it would go on and on,
Now I'm gone,
And the strings were cut
Dragging feelings behind
And feelings wear away
Some day
Like those times spent at the bay
But now you're not in my life
And now I'm gone.
Long Long gone.

January 22, 1990

A Relationship in a Cold Winter

In the morning, after dawn,
When the dew like our tears is dried
My lace and fragrant winter rose wilts
So with both arms I embrace and hold onto dead
Petals that fall on my frost bitten heart brittle
and crumble
And I dream all day until a summer night
When my Angelic Moon will reflect the sun to my
Soul.

January 23,1990

WHY

She is young,
With visions of life,
Her hopes and goals
Are very distant.
She looks for answers
She'll never find.
Thus, I become a teacher,
And tell thee that "why?"
Is grandly a rhetorical question.
If anybody knew the answers
There'd be no reasons for life,
For pursuing the ultimate challenge.
"Reality? Don't question it, it just is."

February 2, 1990

Perspective Blinders

   Doors are meant to be opened, unless they
are locked or have a "do not disturb" sign on
the knob. In this case, a secret is being kept or
someone is displaying an escapist attitude.

Too long in a room without windows
Is like being too long with a mind full of bigotry.
In both one can live,
But both cut one off from experiencing life.

February 7, 1990

WIND

Her midnight eyes
Her misty glance
Her soul shaking smile
She steals my heart
She lights my stars
She blows my mind
Weaving emotions
Look at her.

Sometime in 1990

I am a Collector of Emotion

I am a collector of Emotion,
That which I seek Day and Night.
    I stow it away deep in my mind,
And like an old picture it slowly fades away.
    All is not lost, I have found you,
You have restored colour to my dreams.
    You have added new emotion,
My collection still grows,
        Stronger day and night.

Sometime in 1990